Science

2nd Edition

Cycles

Primary 3 & 4

Activity Book

Tomato seeds

Dr Kwa Siew Hwa • Teo-Gwan Wai Lan
Science Education Consultant: Dr Charles Chew

APPROVED BY MINISTRY OF EDUCATION

for use from 2008-2012

Marshall Cavendish
Education

Preface

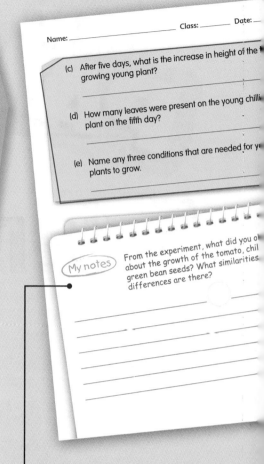

MY PALS ARE HERE! Science Activity Book provides a stimulating, hands-on approach to the learning of Science. Complementing the Textbook, it sets the context for pupils to experience first-hand the process of seeking answers to questions in an exciting and interesting way.

The activities in this book are presented in a variety of formats. There are experiments and investigations, projects and even activities that encourage outdoor exploration.

My notes
Provides opportunities for pupils to reflect and communicate what they have learnt

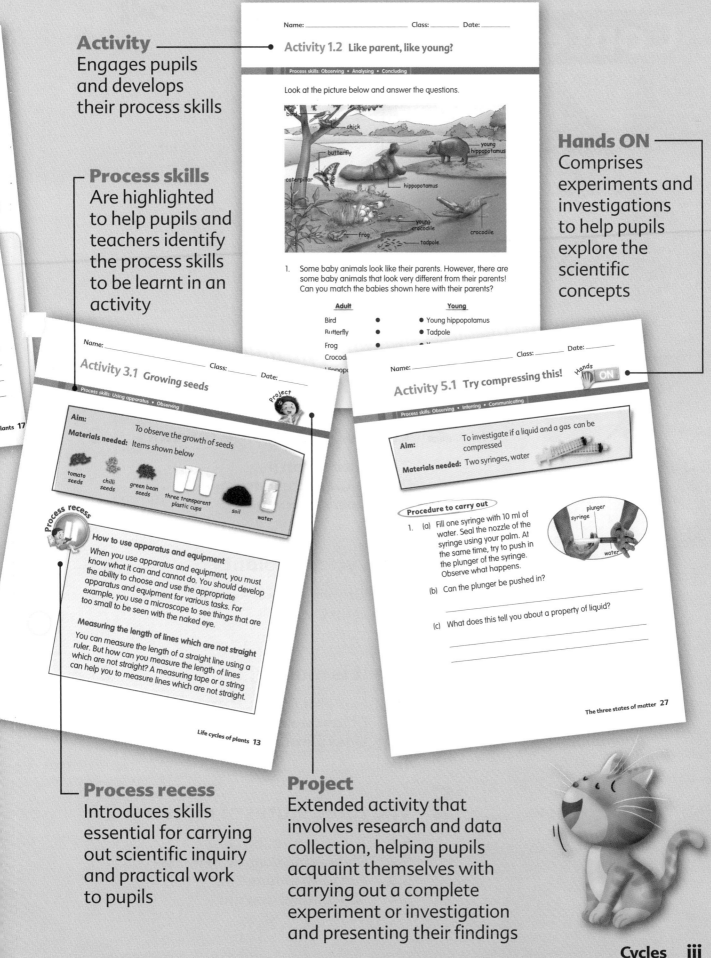

Activity
Engages pupils and develops their process skills

Process skills
Are highlighted to help pupils and teachers identify the process skills to be learnt in an activity

Hands ON
Comprises experiments and investigations to help pupils explore the scientific concepts

Process recess
Introduces skills essential for carrying out scientific inquiry and practical work to pupils

Project
Extended activity that involves research and data collection, helping pupils acquaint themselves with carrying out a complete experiment or investigation and presenting their findings

Name: _____ Class: _____ Date: _____

Activity 1.2 Like parent, like young?

Process skills: Observing • Analysing • Concluding

Look at the picture below and answer the questions.

1. Some baby animals look like their parents. However, there are some baby animals that look very different from their parents! Can you match the babies shown here with their parents?

Adult		Young
Bird	•	• Young hippopotamus
Butterfly	•	• Tadpole
Frog	•	
Crocodile		

Name: _____ Class: _____ Date: _____

Activity 3.1 Growing seeds

Process skills: Using apparatus • Observing

Aim: To observe the growth of seeds
Materials needed: Items shown below

tomato seeds, chilli seeds, green bean seeds, three transparent plastic cups, soil, water

Process recess

How to use apparatus and equipment

When you use apparatus and equipment, you must know what it can and cannot do. You should develop the ability to choose and use the appropriate apparatus and equipment for various tasks. For example, you use a microscope to see things that are too small to be seen with the naked eye.

Measuring the length of lines which are not straight

You can measure the length of a straight line using a ruler. But how can you measure the length of lines which are not straight? A measuring tape or a string can help you to measure lines which are not straight.

Life cycles of plants 13

Name: _____ Class: _____ Date: _____

Activity 5.1 Try compressing this!   Hands ON

Process skills: Observing • Inferring • Communicating

Aim: To investigate if a liquid and a gas can be compressed
Materials needed: Two syringes, water

Procedure to carry out

1. (a) Fill one syringe with 10 ml of water. Seal the nozzle of the syringe using your palm. At the same time, try to push in the plunger of the syringe. Observe what happens.

   (b) Can the plunger be pushed in?
   _____

   (c) What does this tell you about a property of liquid?
   _____
   _____

The three states of matter 27

Cycles   iii

Contents

Cycles

Activity 1.1 It's a match!

Play a matching game. The group which gets the most number of correct matches wins!

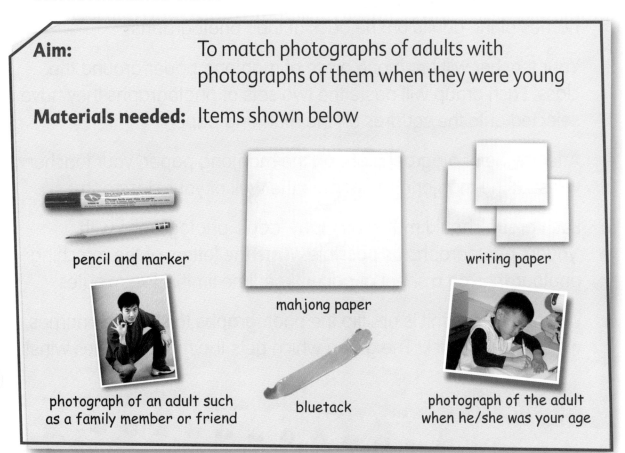

Aim: To match photographs of adults with photographs of them when they were young

Materials needed: Items shown below

pencil and marker

mahjong paper

writing paper

photograph of an adult such as a family member or friend

bluetack

photograph of the adult when he/she was your age

How to observe

When you observe, you use your eyes to see the colour, shape and size of an object. You may use your hands to feel the texture of the object. You may use your ears to listen for any sounds made by the object.

Life cycles 1

1.   Your teacher will separate you into groups. Each group will bring photographs of adults and photographs showing the adults when they were young.

2.   Each group will select two sets of photographs. Each set of photographs should contain one photograph of the adult and one photograph when the adult was young. Use a pencil to write the names of the adults on the back of their photographs.

3.   Your teacher will bring one piece of mahjong paper around the class. Each group will paste the two sets of photographs they have selected onto the squares on the mahjong paper.

4.   After all the photographs are on the mahjong paper, your teacher will stick the mahjong paper onto the wall of your classroom.

5.   Each group should match as many 'adult' photographs with 'young' photographs as possible. Write the letters of the matching photographs on a sheet of paper. The time limit is five minutes.

6.   When the time limit is up, flip the photographs to show the names written on the back. The group which gets the most matches wins!

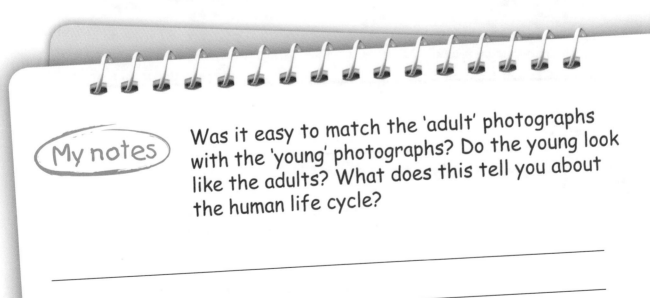

My notes

Was it easy to match the 'adult' photographs with the 'young' photographs? Do the young look like the adults? What does this tell you about the human life cycle?

_____

_____

_____

Activity 1.2 Like parent, like young?

Look at the picture below and answer the questions.

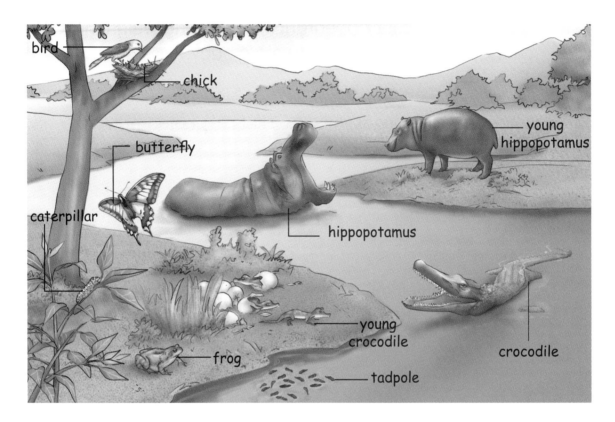

1. Some baby animals look like their parents. However, there are some baby animals that look very different from their parents! Can you match the babies shown here with their parents?

Adult		Young
Bird	●	● Young hippopotamus
Butterfly	●	● Tadpole
Frog	●	● Young crocodile
Crocodile	●	● Chick
Hippopotamus	●	● Caterpillar

2. (a) Name the stages of a human's life cycle.

_____

(b) Which stage are you at now?

_____

(c) Describe how your appearance, height and weight have changed from the time you were a baby.

_____

_____

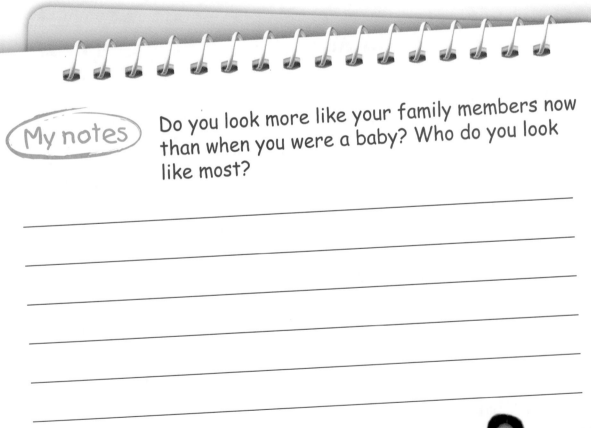

My notes

Do you look more like your family members now than when you were a baby? Who do you look like most?

_____

_____

_____

_____

_____

_____

Activity 2.1 Mealworm pet

Aim: To learn about the life cycle of a beetle

Mealworms are the larvae of a kind of beetle. They are not real worms!

Keep a mealworm and watch it grow. Remember that a mealworm is a living thing with needs. Take care of it properly and watch how it changes!

Procedure to carry out

1. Draw a line to match the needs of the mealworm to the way the needs are met.

Needs of a mealworm	How to meet the needs
Warmth •	• Keep it in a container. Cover the container with a piece of gauze.
Food •	• Give it a slice of an apple or a small piece of fruit.
Water •	• Feed it with bran bought from pet shops. Wholemeal bread and oats can also be given.
Air •	• Keep it in a warm place but away from sunlight.

2. Use a digital camera to take pictures of the mealworm as it grows. Paste the pictures in the spaces below. You may also draw pictures to show the changes.

I obtained my mealworm on _____.

Larva

Date: _____

Larva (two weeks later)

Date: _____

3. Continue to watch your mealworm grow. Take pictures of the mealworm when it turns into a pupa and when it becomes an adult beetle. You may also draw pictures.

Pupa

Date: _____

Adult beetle

Date: _____

4. How many stages are there in the life cycle of a beetle?

_____

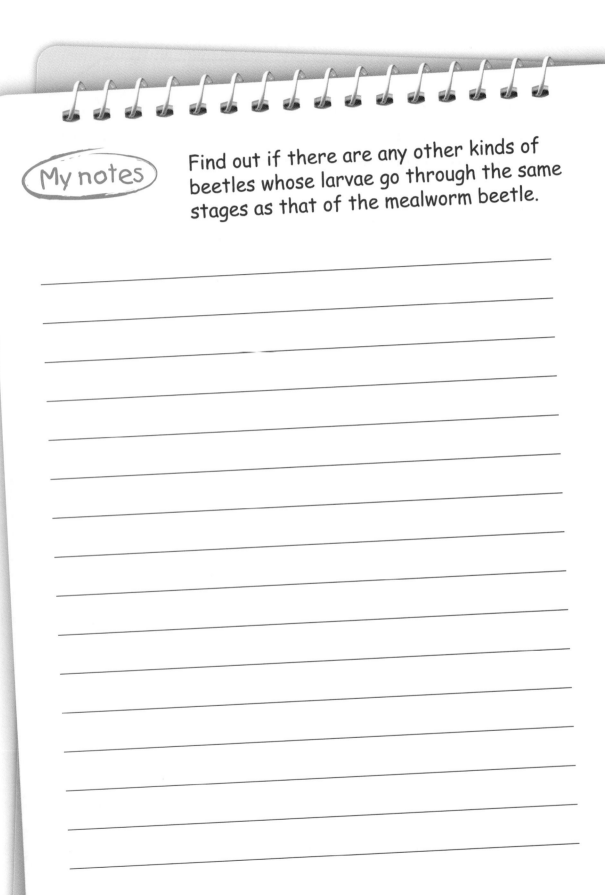

My notes

Find out if there are any other kinds of beetles whose larvae go through the same stages as that of the mealworm beetle.

Activity 2.2 Make a comparison

Compare the young of a butterfly and the young of a cockroach. In what ways are they similar? In what ways are they different?

Process recess

When you are **comparing** things, look for their similarities and differences.

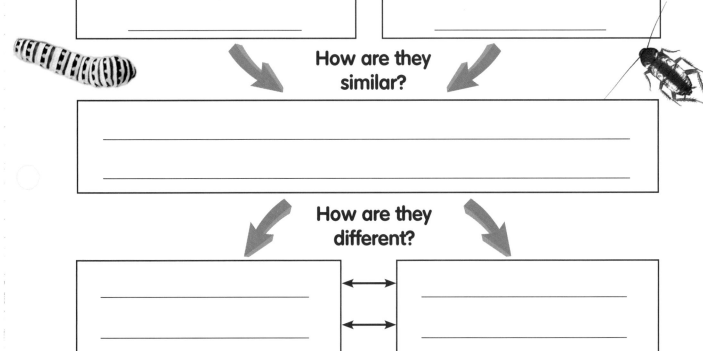

What is the young of a butterfly called?	What is the young of a cockroach called?
_____	_____

How are they similar?

_____

_____

How are they different?

_____	_____
_____	_____
_____	_____
_____	_____

How is the life cycle of a butterfly different from that of a cockroach?

_____

_____

My notes

The life cycles of some insects, such as butterflies, include the pupa stage. The young of these insects do not look like the adult. What do you think happens to these insects at the pupa stage?

_____

_____

_____

_____

_____

_____

_____

_____

_____

_____

Activity 2.3 Busting dengue

There have been mosquitoes breeding around the place you are living in. A few of your neighbours are ill with dengue fever, a disease caused by the *Aedes* mosquito. How can you help to prevent the mosquitoes from breeding?

Aim: To learn about the life cycle of a mosquito and think of ways to prevent mosquitoes from breeding

Procedure to carry out

1. Work in small groups.

2. Research on the life cycle of a mosquito and find out the conditions which it survives in. You may search the Internet or visit the library to find out the information you need.

3. Use the results collected to answer the questions on the next page.

(a) Draw a diagram in the space given to show the life cycle of a mosquito.

(b) Do all the stages of growth of a mosquito occur in dry areas?

_____

(c) What do you see around you that encourage the breeding of mosquitoes?

_____

_____

_____

_____

4. Discuss three ways which will help stop mosquitoes from breeding.

5. Design a poster to present your ideas to your class.

Activity 3.1 Growing seeds

Aim: To observe the growth of seeds

Materials needed: Items shown below

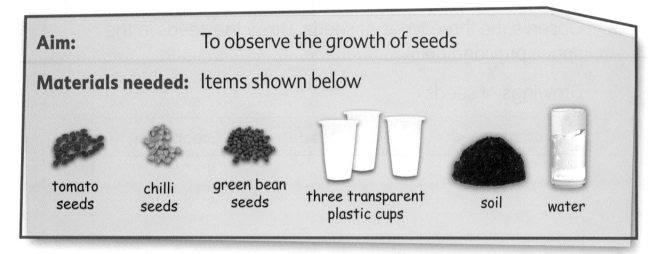

tomato seeds   chilli seeds   green bean seeds   three transparent plastic cups   soil   water

Process recess

How to use apparatus and equipment

When you use apparatus and equipment, you must know what it can and cannot do. You should develop the ability to choose and use the appropriate apparatus and equipment for various tasks. For example, you use a microscope to see things that are too small to be seen with the naked eye.

Measuring the length of lines which are not straight

You can measure the length of a straight line using a ruler. However, how can you measure the length of lines which are not straight? A measuring tape or a string can help you to measure lines which are not straight.

1. Work in small groups.

2. Observe the three types of seeds. Draw the seeds in the space provided below.

    Drawings of seeds

Tomato seed	Chilli seed	Green bean

3. Put some soil in a cup as shown on the right. Sprinkle some water onto the soil.

cup

soil

4. Place three tomato seeds in the soil.

5. Do the same for the chilli seeds and green beans in two other separate cups.

6. Leave the cups in one corner of the classroom. Remember to sprinkle water onto the soil every day to keep it damp at all times.

7. Observe the growth of the seeds into young plants and record your observations in the table on the next page.

Seed	Date when seed was planted	Date when young plant first appeared	Number of days taken for the young plant to appear
Tomato			
Chilli			
Green bean			

8. Wait for the seeds to grow into young plants first. Then use a measuring tape or a ruler to measure the height of the young plants daily for five days.

1. Height of young plant

   Measure the height of each young plant every day at the same time. Start from the day the root first appears (Day 1).

Plant	Height (mm)					
	Day 1	Day 2	Day 3	Day 4	Day 5	Day 6
Young tomato plant						
Young chilli plant						
Young green bean plant						

2. Answer the following questions.

   (a) Which seed was the first to grow?

   _____

   (b) Where does the growing seed get its food from?

   _____

   _____

(c) After five days, what is the increase in height of the fastest growing young plant?

_____

(d) How many leaves were present on the young chilli plant on the fifth day?

_____

(e) Name any three conditions that are needed for young plants to grow.

_____

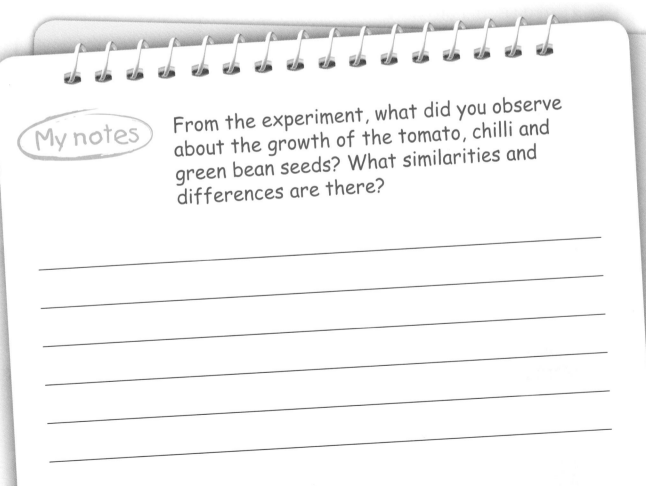

My notes

From the experiment, what did you observe about the growth of the tomato, chilli and green bean seeds? What similarities and differences are there?

_____

_____

_____

_____

_____

Activity 3.2 Help the seed!

The seed below is growing up. However, it does not know what to do. It needs your advice. Help the poor seed grow up into an adult plant!

Please help me grow up into an adult plant!

The growing seed	Your advice
1. I am a seed. I am hard and small. I am ready to grow into a new plant. There is enough air and warmth around me, but that is not enough. What else do I need? Please help me!	
2. I am now ready to start to grow. Which part of me should grow out first? In which direction should this part of my body grow? Why do I need to do this?	
3. I need food to grow. Luckily I have food in store. Do you know where my food is stored?	

The growing seed	Your advice
4. It looks like my store of food is getting low. It is time for another part of my body to grow out. Which part should it be? In which direction should this part of my body grow? Why do I need to do this?	
5. I make my own food and grow. In order to make sure that life continues, I need to do something. What must I do?	

My notes

Find out what the outer covering of a seed is called. Why do seeds have this outer covering?

_____

_____

_____

_____

_____

_____

BLANK

Activity 4.1 Exploring mass

Process skills: Observing • Comparing • Communicating • Inferring

Aim: To compare the mass of different things

Materials needed: Two plastic cups, sand, cotton wool

Procedure to carry out

1. Your teacher will give you a cup of sand and a cup of cotton wool. Both are filled to the same level.

    Pick up the cup of sand and the cup of cotton wool in each hand and compare their masses. Now, imagine your hands to be a lever balance.

cotton wool   sand

(a) How does it feel holding the cup of sand compared to holding the cup of cotton wool? Which hand would go up and which hand would go down?

_____

(b) Which cup has a bigger mass? _____

2. Your teacher will now give you another two cups, each filled with a different amount of sand. Place one cup of sand on each hand.

   (a) Which cup is heavier? _____

   (b) Which cup has a bigger mass? _____

less sand

more sand

Conclusion

The mass of an object depends not only on its _____, but also on the _____ that it is made of.

Activity 4.2 Balancing masses

Aim: To show that smaller amounts of mass can add up to a greater mass

Materials needed: Lever balance, fixed masses of various sizes, small objects such as a plastic pencil case and big objects such as a flower pot

Procedure to carry out

1. Place a 200 g mass on one weighing pan.

2. Place smaller fixed masses on the other weighing pan to balance the 200 g mass.

3. Add up the total mass of the smaller fixed masses.

    What is the value? _____

4. Remove the masses placed on the pan balance in steps 1 and 2.

5. Place a small object on one of the weighing pans.

6. Then make the pans balance by putting some fixed masses on the other weighing pan.

7. Record your observation in the table provided on the next page.

Small object	Total mass of fixed mass used	Mass of the object

8. Place a bigger object on one of the weighing pans.

9. Gather some small objects around you.

10. Predict the objects you would need to balance both pans.

11. Test to see if your prediction is correct. Record your observations below.

Big object	My prediction	My observation
	Objects I think are needed to balance the pans	Did the pans balance? Were there too many, too little or just the right number of objects?

Conclusion

Smaller masses can be _____ up to balance a _____

mass. Objects have _____ no matter how small they are.

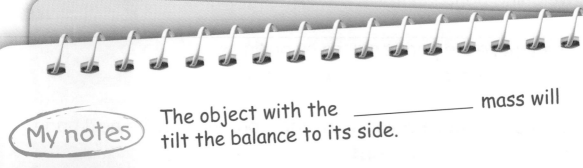

My notes) The object with the _____ mass will tilt the balance to its side.

Activity 4.3 Does air occupy space?

Process skills: Observing • Generating • Communicating • Inferring • Using apparatus

Aim: To show that air occupies space

Materials needed: Tissue paper, deep transparent plastic tub, transparent plastic cup, thumbtack, sticky tape

Procedure to carry out

tissue paper ——

plastic cup ——

Activity A

1. Fill the plastic tub with water.

2. Stick the tissue paper to the bottom of the plastic cup using the sticky tape.

3. Invert the plastic cup and push it into the tub of water. Make sure that the top of the cup is below the water surface in the tub.

Results

Observe the water level in the cup.

Explain why the tissue paper remains dry.

_____

_____

_____

Activity B

thumbtack

1. Use a thumbtack and make a hole at the base of the inverted plastic cup while it is still in the water.

Results

(a) Describe what you see.

_____

_____

(b) Explain why.

_____

_____

My notes

What property of air is shown in activities A and B?

_____

_____

_____

_____

_____

Name: _____ Class: _____ Date: _____

Activity 5.1 Try compressing this!

Aim: To investigate if a liquid and a gas can be compressed

Materials needed: Two syringes, water

___Procedure to carry out___

1. (a) Fill one syringe with 10 ml of water. Seal the nozzle of the syringe using your palm. At the same time, try to push in the plunger of the syringe. Observe what happens.

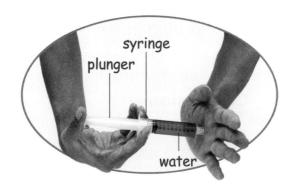

    (b) Can the plunger be pushed in?

    _____

    (c) What does this tell you about a property of liquid?

    _____

    _____

2. Fill a syringe with 10 ml of air. Seal the nozzle of the syringe using your palm. Now push on the plunger lightly, then harder, and then as hard as you can.

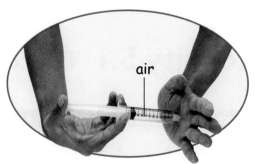
air

(a) What happened to the plunger as you push harder on it?

_____

Now, let go of the plunger.

(b) What happened to the plunger? What can you infer about the volume of air in the syringe?

_____

_____

Conclusion

A _____ cannot be compressed because it has a definite volume. A _____ can be compressed because it has no definite volume.

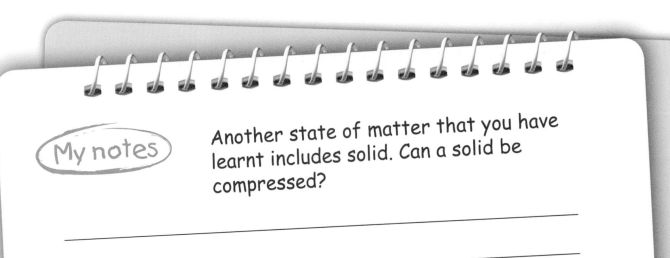

My notes

Another state of matter that you have learnt includes solid. Can a solid be compressed?

_____

_____

Activity 5.2 Measuring volume of liquids

Process skill: Using apparatus

Aim: To find out how to measure the volume of liquids

Materials needed: Items shown below

syringe   beaker   measuring cylinder

Procedure to carry out

1. Find out the maximum volume of liquid each apparatus can contain. Complete the table below.

Measuring apparatus	It can measure volumes up to

2. List the apparatus according to the volume of liquid each can contain, starting from the smallest to the largest.

_____

3. Fill a syringe with 10 ml of water. Transfer the water from the syringe to a measuring cylinder. Then pour the water from the measuring cylinder into a beaker.

Answer the following questions based on your observation.

(a) What changes to the water did you observe when it was transferred into different apparatus?

_____

(b) Can all the three apparatus hold the same maximum volume of water?

_____

(c) Which apparatus would you choose to measure these volumes of liquid?

    (i)   1 ml   : _____

    (ii) 25 ml : _____

    (iii) 80 ml : _____

Activity 5.3 Fun with volume!

Aim: To find the volumes of three different stones

Materials needed: Measuring cylinder, three stones of different sizes, water

Procedure to carry out

1. The space occupied by a stone is called its volume. How do we measure the volume of a stone?

(a) Predict the volume of the stone: _____ ml

(b) Fill a measuring cylinder with 50 ml of water. Record the volume of water in the table below.

(c) Drop the stone gently into the water. Observe what happens to the level of water. Find the total volume of the water and stone by reading the water level. Record your reading in the table below and calculate the volume of the stone.

Volume of water	
Volume of water + stone	
Volume of stone	

Conclusion

The stone takes up _____ and causes the water level to _____.

2. Here is a way you can find the volume of three stones at one go.

   (a) Collect stones of three different sizes. Label them as A, B and C.

stone A   stone B   stone C

   (b) Fill a measuring cylinder with 20 ml of water.
       Record the volume of water in the table on page 33.

   (c) Drop stone A gently into the water. Find the total volume of the water and stone A. Record your reading in the table.

   (d) Next, drop stone B gently into the water. Find the total volume of the water, stone A and stone B. Record your reading in the table.

   (e) Now, drop stone C gently into the water. Find the total volume of the water and all the stones. Record your reading in the table.

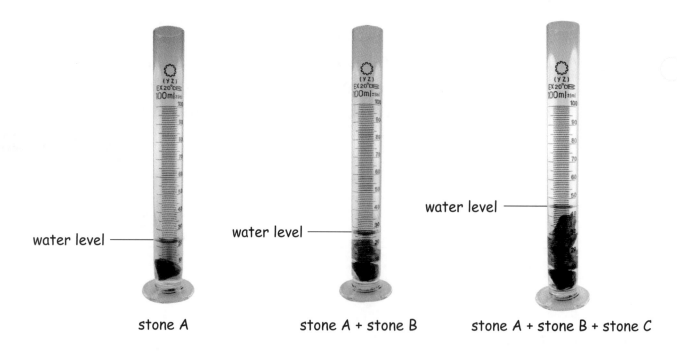

stone A   stone A + stone B   stone A + stone B + stone C

Volume of water	20 ml
Volume of water + stone A	
Volume of water + stone A + stone B	
Volume of water + stone A + stone B + stone C	

(f)   Find the volumes of the stones from your results. Show your steps clearly and include the unit of measurement.

Volume of stone A	
Volume of stone B	
Volume of stone C	

3.   List the stones (A, B and C) in ascending order of their volumes.

_____

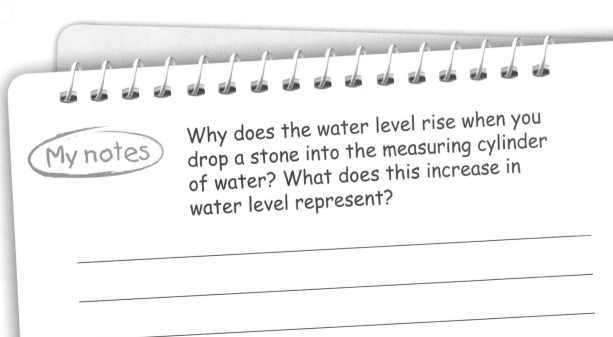

My notes

Why does the water level rise when you drop a stone into the measuring cylinder of water? What does this increase in water level represent?

_____

_____

_____

Activity 5.4 Solid, liquid and gas

A) Jamal's investigation

Jamal has a piece of play dough. He moulds the piece of clay into different shapes. After Jamal moulds each shape, he measures its mass and volume.

1. What is Jamal trying to find out from this activity?

    _____

    _____

2. The table here shows part of Jamal's results. The rest of the table was accidentally torn off. Will you be able to help Jamal re-create his table?

    Draw what the table would look like in the space below and complete it for Jamal.

Shape of clay	Mass (g)	Volume (cm³)
Sphere	65	25
Cube		
Cylinder		

B) A Challenge

Mei Ling and Joel have two containers of the same size. Mei Ling fills up container A with marbles. Joel fills up container B with water.

container A

container B

1. What do you think will happen when Joel pours all the water from container B into container A?

   _____

2. What do you think will happen when Mei Ling pours all the marbles from container A into container B?

   _____

3. What property of matter did you observe from the above experiments?

   _____

BLANK